COLLECTOR'S
CHOICE

7. BRUNETTO LATINI. *Il tesoro*. [Treviso, 1474].

Collector's Choice

A Selection of Books and Manuscripts

Given by Harrison D. Horblit

to the Harvard College Library

A COMMENCEMENT EXHIBITION

FOR THE CLASS OF 1933

THE HOUGHTON LIBRARY

CAMBRIDGE, MASSACHUSETTS

1983

The catalogue was written by Owen Gingerich,
Harvard-Smithsonian Center for Astrophysics

The border on the front cover is taken from item 37:
John Napier, *Mirifici logarithmorum canonis constructio*, Edinburgh, 1619;
and the illustration on page 7 is from item 12:
Honorius Augustodunensis, *Lucidarius* [Strassburg, ca. 1481].

FOREWORD

I N the back of every collector's mind is the question of the ultimate fate of his beloved possessions. The ideal solution, of course, when one passes from this earthly realm, is to "take it with you." Since this has its drawbacks, a second solution might be to "stay with it," which has been rather attractively accomplished in several instances. In my case, a third solution has proven most satisfactory and rewarding—many of my favorite books now reside at Harvard.

The urge to collect works in the history of science was first instilled in me by Professor L. J. Henderson in his sparsely attended "snap" course in the history of science—then the only course on the subject at Harvard. Later, my friendship of many years with Professor William A. Jackson, then Librarian of the Houghton Library, served to fuel my ardor. His knowlege, enthusiasm, and complete dedication to Harvard was an inspiration to me and to many others.

I view the fate of these books as most pleasant—they reside permanently amongst "friends" in a fine physical climate, well cared for, and in an atmosphere of interested and appreciative viewers.

Most of what constitutes Harvard—physically and intellectually—has been made possible by alumni and friends. I am pleased to have joined in this most worthy, continuing effort.

Harrison D. Horblit
Ridgefield, Connecticut
January 1983

5

INTRODUCTION

HARRISON HORBLIT began searching out rare works in the history of science long before it was fashionable to collect early science, and without a guide such as his own Grolier Club volume, *One Hundred Books Famous in Science*. More recently he became intrigued with the pioneering days of photography, and he began to acquire the photographically illustrated books of Fox Talbot long before early photography became fashionable. An admirer of the great nineteenth-century manuscript collector Sir Thomas Phillipps, Horblit gathered together some selected manuscripts and a great deal of memorabilia from Phillipps' remarkable library.

But what characterizes Horblit as a collector as much as his prescient judgement has been the impeccable taste of his selections. Often he has gone for the exquisitely rare, but whenever there was a choice, he has taken a splendid copy that revealed the book as an historical artifact as well as a significant text. "Never say a book is unobtainable," he has often told me, but some of the items he managed to obtain are now essentially unobtainable for anyone else. I think, for example, of the first edition of Robert Recorde's arithmetic, which is known to exist only in a copy at the British Library and in the Horblit copy at Harvard.

A significant number of Horblit's choicest items now reside in Houghton Library. A few, such as the epoch-making first printed description of the heliocentric system, are exhibited nearly every year, when they play a direct role in Harvard undergraduate education. Harvard's oldest important manuscript, presented by Horblit in 1961, is regularly studied by graduate students in paleography. Other volumes, such as the series of small English almanacs, have been examined for at least one doctoral thesis. Still others are sleeping silently in the stacks, awaiting their opportunity to reward some future scholar with the answer to a research problem or with the path to a serendipitous new insight.

This catalogue and exhibition show only a fraction of the treasures that Harrison Horblit has shared with Harvard. His gifts to Houghton Library include forty-one incunabula, volumes from the first half century of printing; sixteen of them are shown here. Of the manuscripts, ranging from what is apparently the earliest papal bull in America (early twelfth century) to a letter from Sigmund Freud on *King Lear*, only two are in the catalogue. Of a large number of "STC" items—English printing before 1641—eleven are included.

On the exhibition labels and in the catalogue that follows, I have tried to indicate the significance of each item either as a text or as an object, or both. It has not been easy to cover such a vast array of learning, so I have borrowed shamelessly from David Eugene Smith's *Rara Arithmetica*, Beaumont New-hall's *Latent Image*, and the *Dictionary of Scientific Biography*. In addition, several members of the Houghton staff including Roger Stoddard, William Bond, and Rodney Dennis have contributed paragraphs. By this catalogue we all express, in small part, our profound gratitude to Harrison Horblit for his generous benefactions. It is our hope that his fiftieth reunion classmates will take some delight in this offering, and that our rival institutions will be suitably jealous!

Owen Gingerich
Professor of Astronomy
and History of Science

1. SAINT AUGUSTINE. *Expositio . . . ex epistola ad Romanos.* [Trier, early ninth century].
(f. 114v. of the Saint Jerome manuscript).

MANUSCRIPTS AND
THE CRADLE OF PRINTING

1 SAINT JEROME. *Explanatio in epistolam Pauli ad Galatas*, etc.
[Trier, early ninth century].

THIS MANUSCRIPT VOLUME, written in Carolingian minuscule script around the
year 810 at the monastery of Saint Maximinus at Trier, contains seven patristic
texts mainly by Jerome, Augustine, and Gregory the Great. The scriptorium of Saint
Maximinus was in close contact with that of Saint Martin's at Tours, and the minuscule
script, which to this day remains the standard form of the roman letter, reached full
development in the two houses at the very time this manuscript was written. During
this period the older half uncial script, also seen here (*see illustration*), was reformed and
brought back into use for chapter headings. The oldest major manuscript in the
Harvard collections, this volume belonged previously to the German Catholic politi-
cian and intellectual Joseph Görres and later to Freiherr von Cramer-Klett.

2 CECCO D'ASCOLI. *L'acerba*. [Italy, ca. 1400].

CECCO D'ASCOLI's encyclopaedic poem in Italian sesta rima discusses the stars,
minerals, and animals and contains in its ninety-sixth chapter a celebrated passage
on the circulation of the blood. Cecco is famous for this poem (which has been
associated with the study of Dante), and for being burned at the stake in Florence in
1327, which raised his status from a rather ordinary astrologer to a martyr of science.
This manuscript was number 4573 in the great collection of Sir Thomas Phillipps.

3 RODRIGO SANCHEZ DE AREVALO. *Speculum vitae humanae.*
[Rome, 1468].

THE SYSTEMATIC PRINTING of books for a cultivated public in Italy began in 1465
when two German printers, Conrad Sweynheym and Arnold Pannartz, set up their
press at a Benedictine monastery in Subiaco. In 1467 they moved to Rome, where they
soon printed this beautiful work so as to appease the powerful and conservative Bishop
Rodricus. Note the spaces for the initials (*see illustration*), which have been splendidly
hand-illuminated in this copy. It is these printers who inspired Johannes Regio-

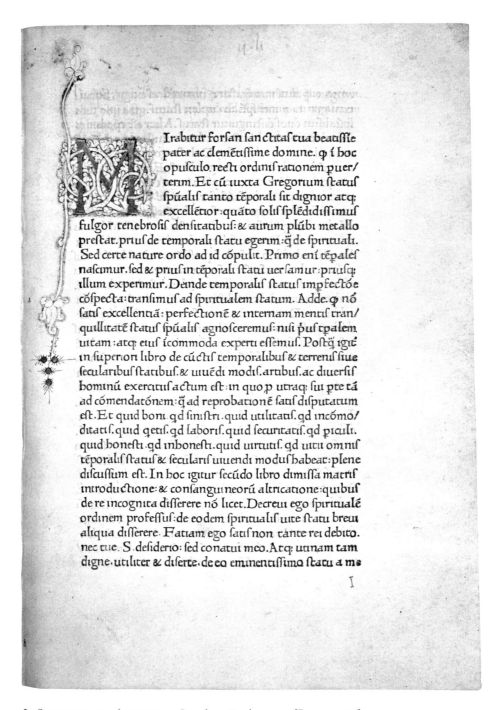

Irabitur forsan san ctitas tua beatissie
pater ac clemetissime domine. op i hoc
opusculo. reeti ordinis rationem puer/
terim. Et cu iuxta Gregorium status
spualis tanto teporali sit dignior atq;
excelletior: quato solis spledidissimus
fulgor tenebrosis densitatibus: & aurum plubi metallo
prestat. prius de temporali statu egerim: q de spirituali.
Sed certe nature ordo ad id copulit. Primo eni tepales
nascimur. sed & prius in teporali statu uersamur: priusq;
illum experimur. Deinde temporalis status imp fecto e
cospecta: transimus ad spiritualem statum. Adde. op no
satis excellentia: perfectione & internam mentis tran/
quillitate status spualis agnosceremus: nisi pust tpalem
uitam: atq; eius icommoda experti essemus. Postq igit
in superiori libro de cuctis temporalibus & terrenis siue
secularibus statibus. & uiuedi modis. artibus. ac diuersis
hominu exercitiis actum est: in quo p utraq; sui pte ta
ad comendatonem: q ad reprobatione satis disputatum
est. Et quid boni. qd sinistri. quid utilitatis. qd incomo/
ditatis. quid qetis. qd laboris. quid securitatis. qd piculi.
quid honesti. qd inhonesti. quid uirtutis. qd uitii omnis
teporalis status & secularis uiuendi modus habeat: plene
discussum est. In hoc igitur secudo libro dimissa matris
introductione: & consanguineoru altricatione: quibus
de re incognita differere no licet. Decreui ego spirituale
ordinem professus: de eodem spiritualis uite statu breui
aliqua differere. Fatiam ego satis non tante rei debito.
nec tue. S. desiderio: sed conatui meo. Atq; utinam tam
digne. utiliter & diserte. de eo eminentissimo statu a me

I

3. SANCHEZ DE AREVALO. *Speculum vitae humanae.* [Rome, 1468].

montanus to add initials of a similar style, but printed from woodblocks, in his own productions in Nuremberg. The Horblit gift includes another important edition from the press of Sweynheym and Pannartz, the 1470 Pliny *Historia naturalis*—a volume too large to show in the exhibition!

4 POMPONIUS MELA. *Cosmographia, sive de situ orbis*. Milan, 1471.

THE ONLY ANCIENT TREATISE on geography in classical Latin, Mela's work of ca. A.D. 43 remained influential until the beginning of the age of exploration. Mela divided the earth into five zones; the two temperate zones were habitable, but the southern one was inaccessible and unknown because of the unbearable heat of the intervening torrid zone. This is the earliest dated printed geography.

5 SAINT ISIDORE OF SEVILLE. *De responsione mundi*. Augsburg, 1472.

IN THIS WORK "on the question of the universe and the arrangement of the stars," the great seventh-century encyclopaedist discusses the divisions of time, the stars, planets, meteorology, earthquakes, volcanoes, and eclipses. A woodblock diagram, displaying the four terrestrial elements, carries the motto "Creation is established from geometrical principles" (*see illustration*).

6 GAIUS JULIUS SOLINUS. *Polyhistor, sive de mirabilibus mundi*. Venice, 1473.

THE *Collectanea* of the third-century geographer and grammarian was revised in the sixth century under the name *Polyhistor*, the form in which it became very popular in the Middle Ages. Largely based on Pliny and in part on Pomponius Mela, it contains a short description of the ancient world with remarks on historical, social, religious, and natural history questions. This is the first printed edition, and the first of many editions of Solinus given by Harrison Horblit to Harvard.

Artes mūdi sunt quatuor·ignis·aer·aqua·terra·qua/
rum haec est natura.Ignis tenuis acutus ac mobilis.
Aer·mobilis acutus & crassus. Aqua crassa obtusa
& mobilis.Terra crassa obtusa immobilis. Quae &iam ita sibi
inuicem cōmiscētur. Terra quidem crassa obtusa & immobilis
cum aquae crassitudine & obtusitate conligatur,Deinde aqua
aeri in crassitudine & mobilitate coniungitur, Rursus aer igni
communione acute & mobili conligatur.Terra autem et ignis
a se separantur sed a duobus mediis aque & aere iungunt.Hec
itaq; ne confusa minus conligatur subiecta expressa sunt figura

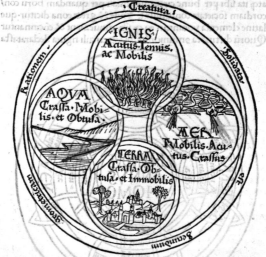

Ceterum sanctus. Ambrosius hec elemēta per qualitates qbus
sibi inuicem quadam nature communione cōmiscentur·ita his
verbis distinguit.Terra inquit arida & frigida est. Aqua frigi
da atq; humida est.Aer calidus & humidus. Ignis calidus est

5. SAINT ISIDORE. *De responsione mundi*. Augsburg, 1472.

7 BRUNETTO LATINI. *Il tesoro*. [Treviso, 1474].

CONTAINING the first printed reference to the nautical compass, this, the earliest book on science in any modern language, treats both physics and zoology. Signore Brunetto was a friend and teacher of Dante; both he and his "Treasury" are mentioned in the *Paradiso*. The Horblit copy, one of only two in America, retains the original fifteenth-century morocco binding with four clasps. (*See frontispiece.*)

8 MARCUS MANILIUS. *Astronomicon*. Nuremberg, [1473/1474].

LITTLE IS KNOWN of Manilius, a Roman writer who flourished at the beginning of the first century A.D. His *Astronomicon*, written in Latin hexameters, is the oldest connected treatise on astrology. This undated first edition was issued by the German astronomer-printer Johannes Regiomontanus, who was influenced by the Renaissance humanistic movement. His use of the new roman types in place of Gothic letters and his pioneering introduction of decorative printed capitals (*see illustration*) represent innovations gleaned from his earlier sojourn in Italy.

9 MARCUS MANILIUS. *Astronomicon*. [Bologna, 1474].

PRINTED in Italy, this edition of Manilius' astrological poem may have preceded the one printed by Regiomontanus (item 8); neither is explicitly dated, and both were published by 1474. In any event, both are available here for study and comparison, thanks to the foresight of the donor. This copy was annotated by the Italian humanist Sebastiano Serico of Saludecio, who included readings from "a most ancient manuscript" (*see illustration*).

F ę mineũ fortita iugum cum pompa rependit
A tꝗ ipfa ifiaco certarunt fulmina fiftro.
R eftabant ꝓfugo feruilia milite bella
Q uom patrios armis imitatus filius hoftis
A equora Pompeius cepit defenfa parenti.
S ed fatis hoc fatis fuerit. iam bella quiefcunt
A tꝗ adamanteis difcordia uincta catenis
A eternos habeat frenos in carcere claufa.
S it pater inuictus patrię. fit roma fub illo.
C um ꝗ deum cęlo dederit non quęrat in orbe;

M. MANILII ASTRONOMICON
SECVNDVS

A ximus iliacę gentis cer/
tamina uates
E t quinquaginta regũ re/
gem ꝗ patrem ꝗ
H ectoream ꝗ facit tutam
fub ꝗ Hectore troiam:
E rrorem ꝗ ducis totidem
quot fecerat annis
I nftantem bello geminata p agmina ponti
V ltima ꝗ in patriam captis ꝗ penatibus arma
O re facro cecinit patria atqui iura petentem
D um dabat eripuit. cuiuf ꝗ ex ore ꝓfufo
O mnis pofteritas latices in carmina duxit.
A mnem ꝗ in tenuis aufa eft deducere riuof
V nius fęcunda bonis. fed ꝓximus illi
H efiodus memorat diuos: diuum ꝗ parentis:

8. MANILIUS. *Astronomicon*. Nuremberg, [1473/1474].

rum asperis linea terre manor ut si linea db X ad ascendens altero
nono ad ascendens d X erit altior q̃ a nono terre vicinor

Nunc tres efficiet:nunc quatuor undicꝫ ductus:
Quos in plura iuuet ratio procedere signa:
Interdum q̃ sint numeris memorata per orbem.
Sed longe maior uis est per signa trigoni:
Quam quibus est titulus sub quarto quocꝫ quadratus
Altior est horum summoto linea templo.
Illa magis uicina meat:cæloꝙ recedit.
Et propius terras accedit uisus eorum.
Aeraꝙ infectum nostras dimittit ad auras:

Euiaꝙ alternis data sunt commertia signis.
Mutua nec magno consensu fœdera seruant:
Inuita angusto q̃ linea flectitur orbe.
Nam cum per tales formantur singula limas
Sydera:& alterno diuertitur angulus astro:
Sexꝙ per anfractus curuatur uirgula in orbem
A tauro uenit in cancrū,tum uirgine tacta
Scorpion ingreditur:qua te capricorne rigentem:
Et geminos a te piscis:aduersaꝙ tauro
Sydera contingens finit:qua cœperat orbem.
Alterius ductus locus & per transita signa.
Vtꝙ ea preteream quæ sunt mibi singula dicta:
Flexibus et totidem similis fit circulus illis:
Transuersos igitur fugiunt subeuntia uisus:
Quod nimis inclinant:ac ne limisꝙ uidentur.
Vicinoꝙ latent.ex recto certior ictus.
Tertia conuerso conduntur signa recessu.
Et quæ succedit connexa linea cælo
Singula circuitu:quæ tantum transeat astra.
Vis eius procul est.altoꝙ uagatur olympo.
Et tenuis uires ex longo mittit in orbem
Sed tamen est illis phœbus sub lege propinquus:
Quod non diuersum genus est:quod euntibus astris
Mascula sed maribus respondent.cætera sexus
Fœminei se coniungunt commertia mundi

10 JOHANNES REGIOMONTANUS. *Disputationes contra Cremonensia deliramenta*. [Nuremberg, ca. 1474].

THE ADVENT of printing provided a powerful force for the reform of astronomy, and no fifteenth-century figure exploited its possibilities more effectively than Johannes Regiomontanus, the first scientific publisher. As a student of the Viennese astronomer Peurbach, he studied Ptolemy's *Almagest*, a work then only imperfectly understood. This dialogue between "Viennensis" and "Cracoviensis," written and printed by Regiomontanus, is a severe critique of the Ptolemaic textbook attributed (falsely) to Gerhard of Cremona. Although long believed to be an example of the new sophistication of Peurbach's school, much of the tract was "borrowed" from a work written a century before by Henry of Langenstein, as recent scholarship has shown.

11 [JACOB PFLAUM?]. *Calendarium*. Ulm, 1478.

THE FIRST printed ephemerides and astronomical calendars were published by Regiomontanus. After his untimely death, the series was revived by Jacob Pflaum of Ulm, beginning in collaboration with the first printer in Ulm, Johann Zainer. This one and only Latin edition, probably compiled by Pflaum, is in a marvelous contemporary wooden binding; it is the earliest of a great variety of almanacs and ephemerides among the Horblit gifts to Harvard.

12 HONORIUS AUGUSTODUNENSIS. *Lucidarius*. [Strassburg, ca. 1481].

ACCORDING to the 1972 census of incunabula, this charming dialogue between a tutor and his pupil is the only copy in America. The "Junger" asks about rivers and rainbows, the places of hell and paradise, and whether everyone will go to heaven. The "Meister" speaks decisively within the framework of a fifteenth-century geocentric universe.

13 JOHANN LICHTENBERGER. *Prognosticatio*. [Ulm, 1488].

HANDSOMELY ILLUSTRATED with an amusing series of woodblocks, this commentary on the foibles of the age went through at least a dozen subsequent editions. The illustration shows two young playboys abandoning their gaming boards for the priesthood. Note that in addition to being tonsured, they are having the fashionable pointed toes of their boots cut off!

Capitulum tricesimúquartú.

Ost hec alius ppheta esurget in terra leonis ↄ in romana curia predicabit mirabília Apparebit sctus ↄ timoraz⁹ sub spé sanctitatis vitá cristianá examinare faciet.mltos pburet igne. In corde suo hébit spiù malignú radicatú q̃ eú sub q̃dá ypocrisi ad summú pótifice ducet licentiá rogitádo Epos ac platos ac pncipes sanctitate ficta decipiet. ↄ ad errore magnú deducet Etiá sapiétisimos errare faciet.mltiↄq̃ famosi viri in italia in longbardia,in alta alemáia decipienf Hic vir erit maior in pplo q̃ vnq̃m aliq̃s a pncipio ecclie bonorat⁹ fuit ↄ vocabit antxps mixt⁹ in pplo.pótifices ip̃m bonorabút.s̃z turpit interficiet ↄ bóies ad scádalú ducent. O si scirent viri enágelici ecclaz rectores huius viri aduentú quó pugnabút aduersus eú ↄ q̃ntá paciens psecutioné.placarét dñm q̃ù flagellú furoris dñi in filios pestilentes erit.clamarent vtiq̃ ↄ pgnoscerent cantore Clamabit verus papa ↄ fiet restauratio noua bona in ecclia post illú. Et ideo si ecclia debeat renouari oportet vt destruat p bunc ppbetam que dissoluta sunt ↄ in peccatis probibentur.

Hic debent comburi alee ↄ vestes seculares difformes rustra caltioↄ iuxta papam abscindi ↄ pili decurticari p bunc ppbetam.

13. LICHTENBERGER. *Prognosticatio*. [Ulm, 1488].

14 LEOPOLD OF AUSTRIA. *Compilatio de astrorum scientia.*
Augsburg, 1489.

PUBLISHED by Erhard Ratdolt, the finest scientific printer of the fifteenth century, this popular handbook of astrological lore features two of the multicolor diagrams that he pioneered. Ratdolt was very likely an apprentice with Regiomontanus in Nuremberg before he set up his own press in Venice, where he introduced a series of important typographic innovations including the modern title page. After he moved to Augsburg astronomical works like this played a diminishing role in his output.

15 *Portolano per tutti i navichanti.* Venice, 1490.

THIS SO-CALLED "portolano Rizo" (named after its publisher) is the earliest printed book on sailing to give distances between ports and islands. The first part includes ports along the English Channel on the route from Flanders to Ireland, and the second includes ports from Venice to Constantinople and Alexandria.

16 BONET DE LATES. *Anuli per eum compositi super astrologiam utilitates.*
[Rome, ca. 1492/1493].

LATES, a Jewish scholar from Provence, tells how to make a circular metal device, reminiscent of an astrolabe, and how to use it to solve a series of astrological problems. As a medical doctor, Lates would have used horoscopes as part of his diagnostic procedure.

17 [JEAN BONNET?]. *Le cuer de philozophie. Translata de Latin en Francoys a la requeste de Philippes le bel Roy de France.* [Paris, ca. 1504].

RICHLY ILLUSTRATED, this exceedingly rare volume by a thirteenth-century Parisian scholar is one of the earliest works on natural science in French (*see illustration*). Printed by Antoine Verard, it contains as the second part what is apparently the earliest translation of Sacrobosco's *Sphere* into any modern language.

habite deuers la.ij⁰.passe la ou le iour est plus long de.xij.heures et bng
quart.La.iij⁰.la ou il a.xij.heures et deux quars / ce est douze heures et
dempe.La.iiij⁰.la ou il pa xij heures et iij quars et aisi ensuiuet en croif
sant le iour a chascune ligne du quart Dune heure iusques a la.xxbi⁰.
ligne/la ou le iour a.xbiij.heures et dempe / et est ce dit ptolomee en la
moindre bretaigne ce est par auanture escoce/ou ce est aucune ligne.Et

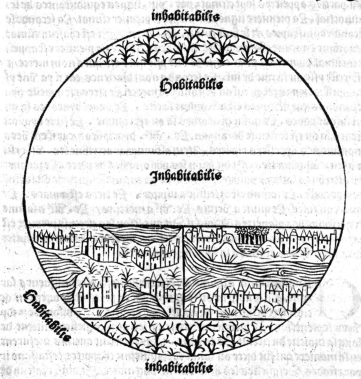

encores met ptolomee habitacion bers septentrion/mais celle habitaciõ
nest pas continuelle/sicomme il note en son quadripertiti/ car comme dit
halp/il a plusieurs lieux inhabitables pour trop grant froit.Par le iour
artificiel on entend le temps de soleil leuant iusques a soleil couchant.
Et par bne heure ie entens la.xxiiij⁰.partie du iour naturel/comme il

17. *Le cuer de philozophie.* [Paris, ca. 1504].

18 JOHANNES DE SACROBOSCO. *Textus de sphera . . . cum additione.*
[Paris, 1494/1495].

SACROBOSCO, a thirteenth-century Augustinian canon, spent most of his life at the University of Paris where he wrote this famous textbook around 1220. At least thirty editions had been printed by 1500 and over one hundred more were printed in the sixteenth century. This 1494 edition is one by Jacques Lefevre d'Étaples, a representative of the new breed of Renaissance editors of the medieval texts.

EARLY ARITHMETICS

19 *Incommincia una practica molto bona et utile . . . vulgarmente larte de labbacho.*
Treviso, 1478.

THIS, the first practical arithmetic to appear in print, was designed to supply the mathematical knowledge necessary for Italian business computations. Multiplication was performed as in modern times until the advent of pocket calculators, but division was undertaken by the "galley" method, so called because the pattern of numbers resembled an ancient galley with its sails set (*see illustration*). Five other copies of this rarity are recorded in American collections.

Et e fatta la rasone. Respondi adoncha. Se lire
1000 de puro valse duc̄ 800 ḡ 16 r̄ i che
varerano lire 14616 ɔ̃re 9 fazi i se. 1

lire 9917.ɛ̃ val. ŭ̃ 800 ḡ 16 r̄ i. 4

Et e fatta. Unde Se lire 1000. e i vɔ canella va

liste ducati 130. e 4 cibe lire 14616 onze 9

La pruova

La terza rasone se forma cosi.
Lire 1000. e i ɔ̃ cɛ̃cula val. ŭ̃ 130. r̄ i. che
varerano lire 14616 ɔ̃re 9 fazi i se. 1

Metti la toa regula in forma cosi.

ducati. 800

19. Arte dell'abbaco. Treviso, 1478.

20 *Ars numerandi.* [Cologne, ca. 1482].

N OT STRICTLY AN ARITHMETIC, this treatise deals with grammatical usage as applied to numbers. Only one other copy of this rare undated incunabulum is found in America. It was probably printed by Ulrich Zell, who had been an apprentice to Fust and Schöffer in Mainz.

21 ÉTIENNE DE LA ROCHE. *Larismethique novellement composee.* Lyon, 1520.

L A ROCHE'S is the first arithmetic in French. David Eugene Smith, the historian of mathematics, has remarked that "perhaps no arithmetic published in France in the sixteenth century gives a more comprehensive view of the science and art of arithmetic and of the applications of the subject." Semi-mercantile in character, it was printed at Lyons, then the commercial center of France.

22 CUTHBERT TUNSTALL. *De arte supputandi libri quattuor.* London, 1522.

I N THE DEDICATION to his friend Sir Thomas More, Tunstall states that he suspected the accounts of certain goldsmiths were incorrect, and so he renewed his study of arithmetic to check their figures. When appointed Bishop of London in 1522 he published these prolix results of his researches, the first arithmetic book to be printed in England.

23 ROBERT RECORDE. *The Ground of Artes Teachyng the Worke and Practise of Arithmetike.* [London], 1543.

T HE FIRST arithmetic book printed in the English language, this truly rare first edition is known in only one other example, in the British Library. As the first commercial arithmetic of any note used in English schools, by 1640 it had passed through twenty-seven further editions. David Eugene Smith has commented that "the language is so formal that it seems strange that the book should have been so successful." In contrast, Joy Easton in the *Dictionary of Scientific Biography* remarks of Recorde that "his use of dialogue enabled him to carry a student step by step through the mastery of techniques; difficult questions were deferred until an understanding of the fundamentals was achieved. . . . Recorde has justly been called the founder of the English school of mathematical writers, and he was also one of the outstanding scholars of mid-sixteenth-century England." (*See illustration.*)

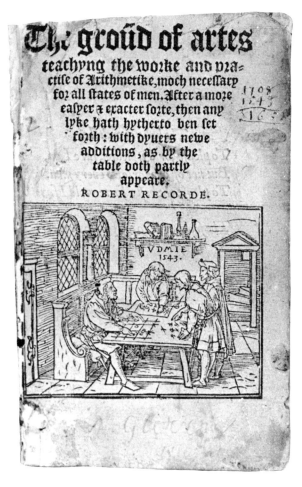

23. RECORDE. *The Ground of Artes*. [London], 1543.

foeuer it be, your quotient fhall beare the fame denomination: precifenes is to be vfed in placing of your triangle, and in meafuring E G and H F, otherwife error may enfue, efpecially if D F be but a fmall diftance, and the angle at B very fharpe, there needeth in this matter no furder admonition, fmall ·practize will refolue all doubtes.

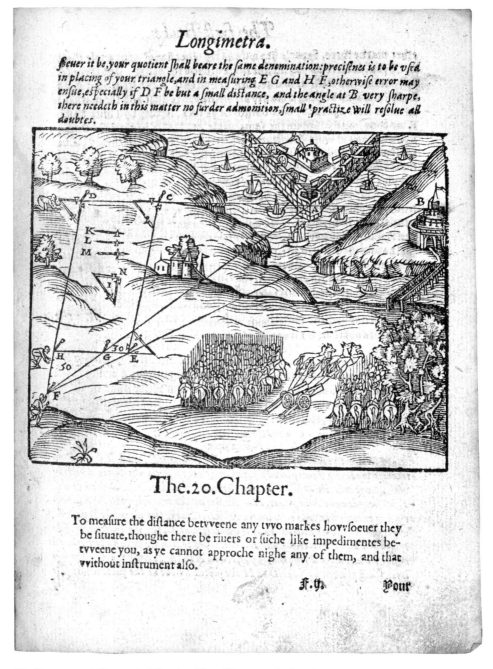

The. 20. Chapter.

To meafure the diftance betvveene any tvvo markes hovvfoeuer they be fituate, thoughe there be riuers or fuche like impedimentes betvveene you, as ye cannot approche nighe any of them, and that vvithout inftrument alfo.

F. ij.   Your

24. DIGGES. *A Geometrical Practise, Named Pantometria.* London, 1571.

EARLY ENGLISH PRINTING

24 LEONARD DIGGES. *A Geometrical Practise, Named Pantometria.*
London, 1571.

THIS WORK, completed by Thomas Digges, contains an intriguing reference to
"marvelouse perspective glasses," perhaps an early reference to the telescope. The
passage mentions "the ayde of glasses transparent, which by fraction should unite or
dissipate the images or figures presented by the reflection of the other." Copiously
illustrated, the *Pantometria* offers practical applications of trigonometry for surveyors
(*see illustration*). This work is representative of Harrison Horblit's special interest in
Digges, father and son.

25 MARCO POLO. *The Most Noble and Famous Travels of Marcus Paulus,
into the East Partes of the World.* London, 1579.

MARCO POLO was the most celebrated European traveler of the Middle Ages. His
importance is not so much due to the considerable length and variety of his
itinerary as to the popularity of his profuse account of his journeys. Upon his return
from Cathay in 1295 Marco met, while in jail, a writer of chivalric romances who
helped him write his story. The account created a sensation. Much of it appeared to be
so fantastic that it was considered fiction, but time has vindicated Marco as a generally
reliable observer. Of this first English translation only half a dozen other copies are
known.

26 [GIORDANO BRUNO]. *La cena de la ceneri.* [London], 1584.

THE "Ash Wednesday Supper," one of six Italian dialogues written by Bruno in
London, is an elaborate metaphor based in part on the Copernican system. In veiled
terms he proposes a religiously liberal alliance between England and France. Along the
way he gives a qualified acceptance of the Copernican system and postulates an infinity
of worlds. The only other copy of this book listed by the National Union Catalogue is
at the University of Southern California.

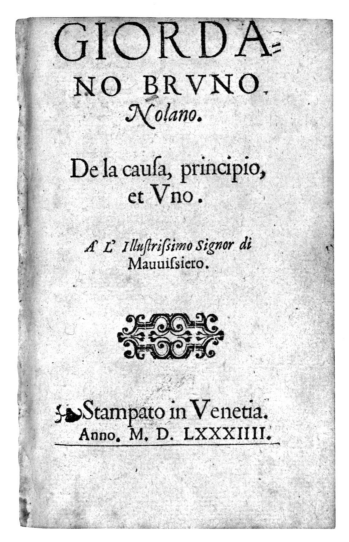

GIORDA-
NO BRVNO.
Nolano.

De la caufa, principio, et Vno.

A' L' Illuftrifsimo Signor di
Mauuifsiero.

Stampato in Venetia.
Anno. M. D. LXXXIIII.

27. Bruno. *De la causa, principio, e uno.* [London], 1584.

27 GIORDANO BRUNO. *De la causa, principio, e uno.* [London], 1584.

HERE BRUNO DESCRIBES the angry protests aroused by his attack on two Oxford "pedants" in his "Ash Wednesday Supper," offering an apology of sorts. His basic theme, however, is an expression of his vision of an infinite spirit pervading an infinite universe. Note on the title page (*see illustration*) the false Venetian imprint of this Italian-language book, which was actually printed in London.

28 LEONARD MASCALL. *A Profitable Booke Declaring Dyvers Approoved Remedies, to Take Out Spottes and Staines . . . with Divers Colours How to Die Velvets . . . also to Dresse Leather.* London, 1588.

THIS "very profitable" English book gives recipes for, among other things, keeping out moths (using "powder of drye Orange Pilles and the powder of Elecompane rootes mixte togeather"), dying leather, hardening tools, and gilding metals. Only three other perfect copies of this edition are known. The fine modern red morocco binding with gold-stamped dentelles is by Rivière.

29 [FEDERICO DI VINCIOLO]. *New and Singular Patternes & Workes of Linnen.* London, 1591.

EXCEPT FOR SOME FRAGMENTS in the British Library, this is the only known copy of this English edition of a French pattern book. The designs are for needlework "to satisfy the gentle mindes of virtuous women." The subtitle offers "the seaven Planets, and many other Figures serving for Patternes to make divers sortes of Lace." The grid on the devices facilitates the transfer or scaling of the pattern (*see illustration*).

30 JOSEPH MOXON. *Practical Perspective: or Perspective Made Easie.* London, 1670.

THE FIRST BOOK to be set in Moxon's own type, and his best piece of printing, the *Practical Perspective* was "usefull for all Painters, Engravers, Architects, &c. and all others that are any waies inclined to Speculatory Ingenuity." Particularly unusual is the fold-out figure and mica window (*see illustration*).

M 3

Venus.

29. [VINCIOLO]. *New and Singular Patternes & Workes of Linnen*. London, 1591.

28

30. MOXON. *Practical Perspective*. London, 1670. (p. 7).

32. Rheticus. *Narratio prima.* Gdansk, 1540.

31 EDWARD SHERBURNE. *The Sphere of Marcus Manilius Made an English Poem: with Annotations and an Astronomical Appendix.* London, 1675.

ALTHOUGH this sumptuous volume contains an English verse translation of Manilius' astrological poem, its real interest lies in the biographical and historical appendix, which constitutes the first history of science in English. Here are found splendid engravings to illustrate the various world systems and descriptions of the work of scores of astronomers. Particularly remarkable is the long notice given to Isaac Newton twelve years *before* the publication of his *Principia*. This large-paper presentation copy is inscribed by Sherburne to Lord Viscount Brounker, the first president of the Royal Society.

THE SCIENTIFIC RENAISSANCE

32 GEORG JOACHIM RHETICUS. *Narratio prima.* Gdansk, 1540.

IT IS POSSIBLE that Rheticus, a young Wittenberg mathematics professor, first heard about the unpublished Copernican theory from Johann Schöner in Nuremberg. At any rate, soon after the twenty-five-year-old Rheticus began his visit to the sixty-seven-year-old Copernicus, he was permitted to publish this "first narrative," the earliest printed account of the heliocentric system, which he dedicated to Schöner. The Horblit copy is bound with a collection of five other sixteenth-century works, and on one of the pages a manuscript horoscope of Johann Schöner appears. About twenty copies of this first edition are known; it is so rare that, for example, no copies are recorded in the British Isles and only one in all of France. According to recent auction records, this first edition of *Narratio prima* is the most valuable printed book in the history of science. (*See illustration.*)

33 NICOLAUS COPERNICUS. *De lateribus et angulis triangulorum.* Wittenberg, 1542.

THE TECHNICAL NATURE of *De revolutionibus* placed it beyond the capabilities of the printers in the university town of Wittenberg; nevertheless, Rheticus succeeded in issuing there its two mathematical chapters for use as a textbook. Hence this trigonometry is Copernicus' first printed scientific work. Like most of the ephemeral textbooks from this period, *De lateribus* is quite scarce, and there are only half a dozen other copies in America.

34 GEORG JOACHIM RHETICUS. *Ephemerides novae.* Leipzig, 1550.

ALTHOUGH Copernicus' *De revolutionibus* boasted on its title page that the reader could easily use its tables to find the planetary positions for any time past or future, such calculations were in fact tedious to carry out. Here Copernicus' disciple Rheticus has calculated positions day by day for the year 1551, the first and only such printed almanac based strictly on the new Copernican tables.

35 JOHANN KEPLER. *Antwort auff Röslini Discurs von heutiger Zeit beschaffenheit.* Prague, 1609.

HARVARD has always had the finest collection of Kepler holdings in America, and this volume has helped the University maintain its impressive lead. It contains the unique copy in America not only of this attack on astrology, but also of the *Bericht vom Geburtsjahr Christi*, Kepler's definitive vernacular statement of his belief that Christ had actually been born in 5 B.C. rather than in A.D. 1. In the "Answer to Röslein," Kepler with "frank German talk" systematically disposes of his countryman's prognostications concerning a universal catastrophe. This tract volume was formerly in the Prince of Liechtenstein's library and later in the collection of Robert Honeyman.

36 JOHN NAPIER. *Mirifici logarithmorum canonis descriptio.* Edinburgh, 1614.

THE GENERAL IDEA of substituting addition and subtraction for tedious multiplication and division was "in the air" in the late sixteenth century, and hints of such a possibility had reached Lord Napier through the Edinburgh physician John Craig, who had taught on the continent for many years. Napier's "Wonderful Table of Logarithms" establishes his priority in what has been acclaimed as the second most important work in the history of the exact sciences to have been published in Great Britain, the first of course being Newton's *Principia*. This thin quarto volume contains fifty-seven pages of description, and ninety pages of tables giving seven-place logarithms of sines for each minute of arc. (The decorative border from the title page of this work has been used as the cover of our catalogue.)

37   JOHN NAPIER. *Mirifici logarithmorum canonis constructio.* Edinburgh, 1619.

NAPIER chose not to describe his method of calculating the logarithms themselves in the *Descriptio*, preferring to wait to see if they actually had practical usefulness. The computational procedure appeared posthumously in this volume, a work that had been written over the years and which, therefore, allows historians to guess how Napier may have originally developed his method of multiplication and division through simple addition and subtraction.

38   JOHN NAPIER. *A Description of the Admirable Table of Logarithmes.* London, 1618.

THE SYSTEM used in the *Mirifici logarithmorum* volumes is neither the common base-ten logarithms nor the natural or so-called Napierian logarithms, but rather to the base $1/e$. On the last page of this work Napier promises to develop a more convenient system. Henry Briggs, the Gresham Professor of Geometry at Oxford and the former owner of this particular copy of the second English edition, noticed a more felicitous scheme, and after consultation with Napier in the summers of 1614 and 1615 proceeded to work out the base-ten logarithms, which he ultimately published in 1624.

39   JOHANN KEPLER. *Ephemerides novae motuum coelestium.* Linz, 1617–1630.

AS SOON AS Kepler saw Napier's *Mirifici logarithmorum*, he understood the significant simplification they offered for the time-consuming tasks of astronomy, such as this daily series of planetary positions. In his enthusiasm, he dedicated these ephem-

33

erides to Baron Napier. Eventually Kepler developed and used his own system of logarithms in his Rudolphine Tables. "It is better," said Kepler quoting Ovid, "for the farmer to set before his guests the produce from his own garden."

40 PHILIP VAN LANSBERG. *Triangulorum geometriae libri quatuor.* Leiden, 1591.

ALTHOUGH Lansberg showed rather little originality in this, his first mathematical work, his arrangement of material was more systematic than that of his rivals, and Kepler found the trigonometrical tables in the second part of the work useful for his astronomical calculations. This is a presentation copy to Landgrave William of Hesse, containing one of the rare specimens of the author's handwriting; it came via the Nordkirchen library.

PRINTING AND BIBLIOGRAPHY

41 ROBERT CLAVEL. *A Catalogue of All the Books Printed in England since the Dreadful Fire of London, in 1666. To the End of Michaelmas Term, 1672.* London, 1673.

THIS bookseller's reference work contains titles, publishers, and prices for six years of English printing, arranged by subject from Divinity through Physick (medicine) and Law, to Poetry and Plays. Nearly a score of navigation books and sixteen arithmetics are listed at prices ranging from 8 pence to 14 shillings. Included at 3s 6p is the next item, Leybourn's *Geometricall Exercises.*

NINE

GEOMETRICALL

EXERCISES,

Jo: Ope

FOR

Young Sea-men,

And others that are studious in

MATHEMATICALL PRACTICES:

Containing IX *particular* TREATISES, *whose* Contents *follow in the next Pages.*

All which EXERCISES are *Geometrically* performed, by a Line of *Chords* and *equal Parts*, by waies not usually known or practised. Unto which the *Analogies* or *Proportions* are added, whereby they may be applied to the *Chiliads* of *Logarithms*, and *Canons* of *Artificiall Sines* and *Tangents*.

By *William Leybourn*, Philomath.

LONDON,

Printed by *James Flesher*, for *George Sawbridge*, living upon *Clerken-well-green*. *Anno Dom.* 1669.

A 2

Vera Effigies Gulielmi
Leybourn. Philom. *anno Ætatis* 30
R. Gaywood fecit.

42. LEYBOURN. *Nine Geometricall Exercises for Young Sea-men.* London, 1669.

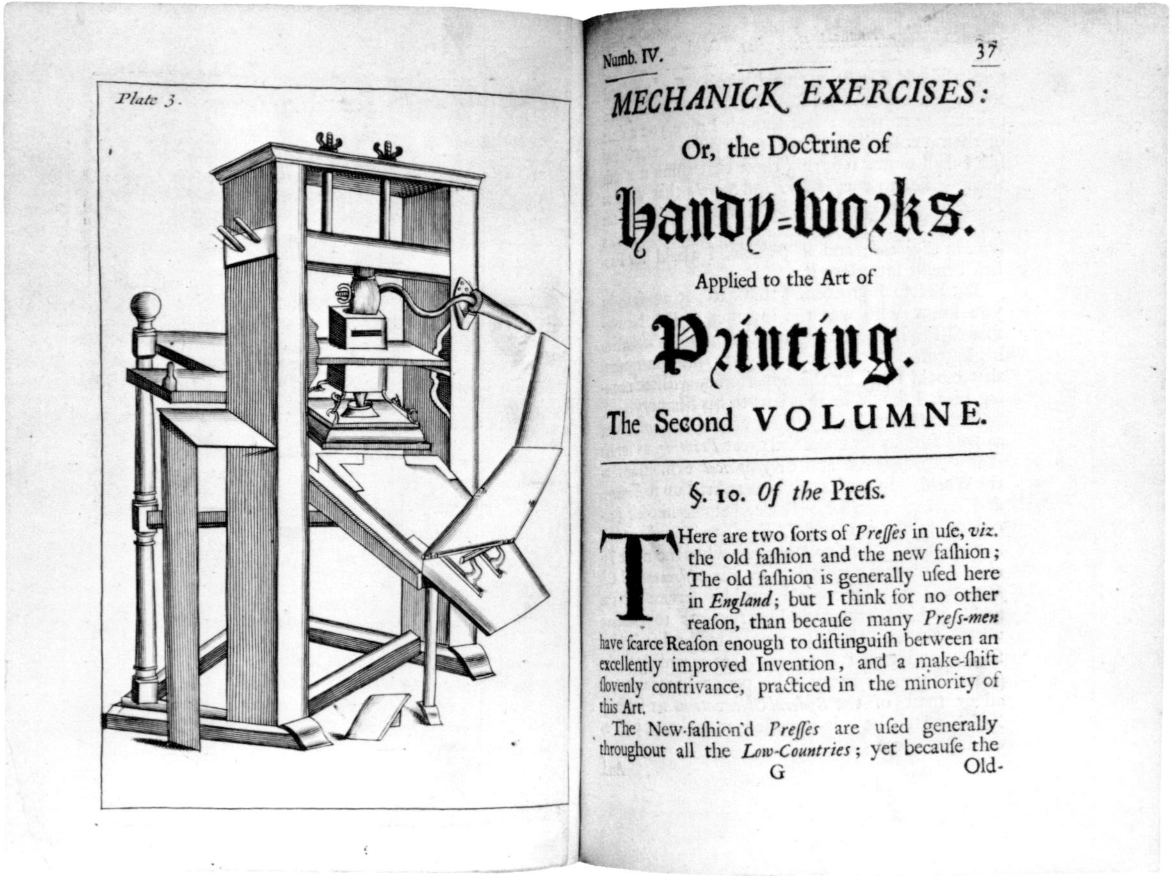

Numb. IV.

MECHANICK EXERCISES:

Or, the Doctrine of

Handy-works.

Applied to the Art of

Printing.

The Second VOLUME.

§. 10. *Of the* Press.

THere are two sorts of *Presses* in use, *viz.* the old fashion and the new fashion; The old fashion is generally used here in *England*; but I think for no other reason, than because many *Press-men* have scarce Reason enough to distinguish between an excellently improved Invention, and a make-shift slovenly contrivance, practiced in the minority of this Art.

The New-fashion'd *Presses* are used generally throughout all the *Low-Countries*; yet because the Old-

G

Plate 3.

43. MOXON. *Mechanick Exercises.* London, 1677[-1683]. 2 v. in 1.

42 WILLIAM LEYBOURN *Nine Geometricall Exercises for Young Sea-men.*
London, 1669.

ORIGINALLY A PRINTER, Leybourn gradually devoted himself to being a "mathe-matical practitioner," and he was one of the surveyors of London following the Great Fire. Of this book, he says, "I thought good to publish something useful and beneficial to English Navigators." The book, a fine example of early English scientific printing and of Harrison Horblit's interests in navigation, is placed here (after the Clavel price list) because it carries the manuscript notation of a contemporary price of 4 shillings, apparently including a dealer's markup of 6 pence! (*See illustration.*)

43 JOSEPH MOXON. *Mechanick Exercises, or, The Doctrine of Handyworks.*
London, 1677[–1683]. 2 v. in 1.

PART II of Joseph Moxon's *Mechanick Exercises* is the earliest fully explanatory treatise in any language on the art of printing. As such it is the starting point for most inves-tigations of early printing. Since the press and its use did not really begin to change until 1800, his book remains a sound guide well into the nineteenth century, and working presses have been built according to his directions in modern times (*see illustration*). Moxon was also a noted maker of scientific instruments from telescopes to sets of Napier's bones, and a hydrographer producing maps, charts, and globes. This scarce volume was Horblit's first gift to Houghton, presented in 1945.

44 [JOHANN HEINRICH GOTTFRIED ERNESTI]. *Die wol-Eingerichtete Büchdrückerey.* Nuremberg, 1721.

LIKE MOXON, Ernesti was a practical printer. His treatise touches all aspects of the art and includes biographies of early printers. It closes with the text of a German comedy about printing and a selection of verse on typographical subjects by Johann Rist. (*See illustration.*)

45 [ROBERT HARDING EVANS]. *Catalogue of a Very Curious and Valu-able Collection of Foreign Books and Manuscripts Recently Consigned from Madrid.* London, 1826.

INTERLEAVED with buyers' names and prices, this copy belonged to one of the most remarkable collectors of all time, Sir Thomas Phillipps, who suspected that his agent Thomas Thorpe had bought the contents in Madrid and consigned them anony-mously. Nonetheless, as he noted on the title page, "Those marked TP I sent for."

Die
Wol-eingerichtete Büchdrückerey,

mit hundert und achtzehen
Teutsch- Lateinisch- Griechisch- und Hebräischen
Schrifften,
vieler fremden Sprachen Alphabeten, musicalischen Noten, Calender-Zeichen,
und Medicinischen Characteren,
Ingleichen
allen üblichen Formaten
bestellet,
und
mit accurater Abbildung der Erfinder der löblichen Kunst,
nebst einer
summarischen Nachricht von den Buchdruckern in Nürnberg,
ausgezieret.
Am Ende ist das gebräuchliche DEPOSITIONS-Büchlein angefüget.

Nürnberg, gedruckt und zu finden bey Johann Andreä Endters seel. Sohn und Erben. 1721.

44. [ERNESTI]. *Die wol-Eingerichtete Büchdrückerey*. Nuremberg, 1721.

46 THOMAS THORPE. *Part I.—1825. A Catalogue of an Extensive Collection of Rare and Curious Books.* London, 1825.

THIS IS A SAMPLE VOLUME from Sir Thomas Phillipps' set of Thorpe's catalogues, bristling with his annotations. The Phillipps-Horblit series, filling several shelves in the Houghton stack, is a major record of the collecting activities of the world's greatest private collector of manuscripts.

SOME INTERESTING BINDINGS

47 TOMMASO DE' MEDICI. *Personal account book.* 1578–1583.

A DISTANT COUSIN of Cosimo, Tommaso here neatly records a multitude of payments to family, retainers, and others. The stiff brown morocco wrap-around binding has five blind-tooled straps laced across the back, the center one continuing around the flap. Such covers, more like saddlery than bookbinding, were reserved for account books (*see illustration*).

48 CRISPIJN VAN DE PASSE. *Effigies regum ac principum.* Cologne, 1598.

THE FINE ENGRAVED PORTRAITS in this rare collection show the most important rulers of the time as well as the explorers Columbus (*see illustration*), Amerigo Vespucci, Magellan, Pizarro, and Sir Francis Drake. Three ships, two constellation maps, and a world map reduced from Mercator's Atlas of 1587 complete the ensemble. The red gold-stamped morocco binding is by Rivière and Sons.

47. Tommaso de' Medici. *Personal account book.* 1578–1583.

CHRISTOPHORVS COLVMBVS GENVENSIS PRIMVS NOVARVM TERRARVM DETECTOR ✝

NOVA DVM BONA

Christophorus genuit quem Genua clara Columbus
(Numine perculsus quo nescio) primus in altum
Descendens pelagus, Solem versusque cadentem
Directo cursu, nostro hactenus abdita Mundo
Littora detexi, Hesperio paritura Philippa :
Audenda hinc alijs plura et maiora relinquens.

48. CRISPIJN VAN DE PASSE. *Effigies regum ac principum*. Cologne, 1598.

49A JOHN GADBURY. *Ephemeris: or, a Diary . . . for the Year . . . 1672.*
[London, 1672].

49B JOHN PARTRIDGE. *Merlinus Liberatus: Being an Almanack for the Year
. . . 1692.* London, [1692].

THESE TWO seventeenth-century almanacs are typical of a long series in the Horblit
gift, which has provided the grist for several scholarly studies at Harvard.
Each volume contains about a dozen small almanacs for a given year. Occasionally gold
stamped with the royal monogram and crowns, these books furnish fine examples of
contemporary binding. Gadbury was one of the most prolific almanac makers of his
day, though his computing abilities are doubtful since his larger volumes of ephemerides were almost entirely pirated from continental tables. Partridge is remembered
today mostly because of a satirical attack by Jonathan Swift, who predicted Partridge's
demise and who subsequently published an obituary for the hapless astrologer, who
was hard put to convince the public that he was still alive!

50 JACQUES LE ROYER. *Oeuvres.* Avranches, 1678.

THE HORBLIT COPY of this wide-ranging treatise on astrology and what would
today be called "water-witching" is remarkable for its unusual printed vellum
sundial binding. It came from the library of the seventeenth-century French polymath
Pierre Daniel Huet.

51 *Almanach royal, annee M.DCC.LVII.* Paris, 1757.

HANDSOMELY BOUND in brown morocco and stamped elaborately in gilt, this
copy bears the arms of its original owner, René-Charles de Maupeou, Marquis de
Mornagles, Vicomte de Bruyères. It was later owned by the great American connois-
seur Lucius Wilmerding.

52 JOHN KNOWLES. *An Inquiry into the Means Which Have Been Taken to
Preserve the British Navy, from the Earliest Period to the Present Time,
Particularly from that Species of Decay, now Denominated Dry-rot.*
London, 1821.

THE H.M.S. *Queen Charlotte* was launched in May 1810, and by July 1811 her officers
discovered that she was "in a state of rapid decay." Knowles' survey resulted from
the ensuing investigation. This is the magnificently bound copy presented by the
author to Tsar Alexander I of Russia.

EARLY PHOTOGRAPHY

53 DOMINIQUE FRANÇOIS JEAN ARAGO. "La daguerréotype." In *Comptes rendus hebdomadaires des séances de l'Académie des sciences*. Vol. 9. Paris, 1839.

ON 6 January 1839 a Paris newspaper announced Daguerre's remarkable discovery of how to fix images on a silver plate, but without giving any technical details. Daguerre knew that if he obtained a patent, anyone could benefit from his secret. Arago was Director of the Paris Observatory, Permanent Secretary of the French Académie des sciences, and a member of the Chamber of Deputies, and hence in an ideal position to sponsor Daguerre in a campaign for direct compensation from the French government. Arago himself learned to make daguerreotypes, so he spoke with authority when he first partially revealed the secrets of photography at the 7 January session of the Academy, here recorded in the Academy's volume of proceedings.

54 HENRY FOX TALBOT. *Some Account of the Art of Photogenic Drawing*. London, 1839.

CHALLENGED by the news from Paris of Daguerre's discovery, Talbot rushed to establish a claim to priority; his account of experiments going back to 1834 was reported to the Royal Society on 31 January 1839. This fourteen-page pamphlet, reprinted by Talbot for private distribution, is the world's first separate publication on photography.

55 LOUIS JACQUES MANDÉ DAGUERRE. *History and Practice of Photogenic Drawing on the True Principles of the Daguerreotype*. London, 1839.

IN AUGUST of 1839 the French Chamber of Deputies voted a life pension for Daguerre in return for the details of his process, which were described to the Academy on 19 August 1839. Before the year was out his directions had become available in seven languages. This is the first English edition of Daguerre's booklet.

56 HENRY FOX TALBOT. *The Pencil of Nature*. London, 1844.

THE GREAT ADVANTAGE of Talbot's negative-positive process (in contrast to the daguerreotype) was that multiple copies could be made from a single master negative. Talbot himself produced this, the first photographically illustrated book. The twenty-four plates comprise views and records of Lacock Abbey, Talbot's home near Bath (*see illustration*). Shown in the exhibit are the first pair of six installments. Between 15 April and 25 May 1844, a thousand prints were made by the Reading Talbotype establishment for the five plates in the first issue of *The Pencil of Nature*.

57 HENRY FOX TALBOT. *Sun Pictures in Scotland*. London, 1845.

TALBOT'S second photographic book, issued in a small edition with just over 100 subscribers, contained twenty-three prints. *Sun Pictures in Scotland* represented Abbotsford and other "scenes connected with the life and writings of Sir Walter Scott" and was published without any text. (*See illustration.*) So unusual was the new photographic technique that Talbot included a small *Notice to the Reader*: "The plates of the present work are impressed by the agency of Light alone, without any aid whatever from the artist's pencil. They are the sun-pictures themselves, and not, as some persons have imagined, engravings in imitation."

56. TALBOT. *The Pencil of Nature*. London, 1844.

57. TALBOT. *Sun Pictures in Scotland*. London, 1845.

Printed by The Stinehour Press and The Meriden Gravure Company
Designed by Stephen Harvard